The Lean Kōhai

This book consists of 76 statements on various issues and practices encountered by process improvement/operational excellence (PI-OpEx) practitioners, managers, and leaders. Many of these issues are also encountered by those outside of PI-OpEx. This book contains instructions, encouraging readers to write and journal in its pages. The key benefits of this work fuel the unending learning journey of PI-OpEx practitioners and leaders.

Practitioners face issues regarding practice, methods, leadership, management, and purpose. The reflections in this book allow them to either tackle the issue upfront and be prepared or the reflections can act as jump-off points to develop an approach to an issue encountered, individually or as a team. For example, the practitioner may have a problematic team member, and using a reflection from the book and having the group discuss it may resolve the issue. Or, the practitioner can read a reflection and use their response to develop a strategy for handling the team member.

Essentially, this book provides readings that could form the basis of daily meditation, be consulted for perspective when a specific issue arises, or both. It seeks to instill a mindset of emotional intelligence that can then fuel the pursuit of meaningful, lasting change.

The Lean Kōhai

Meditations for Strategy, Practice, and Balance in Living Change Management

Don Arp, Jr.

A PRODUCTIVITY PRESS BOOK

First published 2025
by Routledge
605 Third Avenue, New York, NY 10158

and by Routledge
4 Park Square, Milton Park, Abingdon, Oxon, OX14 4RN

Routledge is an imprint of the Taylor & Francis Group, an informa business

ISBN: 9781032830292 (hbk)
ISBN: 9781032830285 (pbk)
ISBN: 9781003507383 (ebk)

DOI: 10.4324/9781003507383

Typeset in Minion
by codeMantra

Dedication

Theodore Roosevelt

'Far and away the best prize that life offers is the chance to work hard at work worth doing'.

'It is only through labor and painful effort, by grim energy and resolute courage, that we move on to better things'.

Contents

Tool: Know Your Path

Tool: Pocket Cards

Tool: Impact Matrix

Tool: Envision Your Customer

Tool: Grief and Change

Tool: Force Fields

Tool: Team-Centered Leadership

Tool: Visualize Everything

Tool: 'Firefighting'—Rapid Reaction Change

Tool: Change Perspective

About the Author

Don Arp, Jr., PhD, is a writer, researcher, and leader, with years of experience in public and private sector compliance, oversight, investigations, operational excellence, management assessment, and executive leadership. Don is a Certified Lean Six Sigma Black Belt and has had his work published in *Six Sigma Forum Magazine* and *Lean & Six Sigma Review.*

Introduction

Managing change is to harness the power of a most human talent—creativity—while mitigating a litany of negative forces, all for the purpose of realizing a better operational state than the one that you have.

In pursuing and delivering change and the management thereof, I advocate for a holistic frame of thought that helps ground the practitioner in a user-focused worldview aimed at achieving the best results possible in complicated operational environments. This book provides readings that could form the basis of daily meditation, consulted for perspective when a specific issue arises, or both. This book seeks to instill a mindset of emotional intelligence that can then fuel the pursuit of meaningful, lasting change.

Each item builds on the other, helping the practitioner create a mature, emotionally grounded approach to change management, leadership, and organizational improvement. It also imparts the lesson that this personal development is never finished and that while the reader will be exposed to various teachings, learning is never complete for the skilled practitioner.

There is a lot of open space on each page, for a reason. WRITE IN THIS BOOK! PLEASE! Treat this book as a development journal. Each reflection has space for Personal Reactions. Write down what you thought of the statement, how it can help you, a quote or life experience it reminds you of . . . literally anything and everything. If you do not like writing, sketch your thoughts. Record your thoughts even if you do not agree with the statement. Further, add your own reflections as you live the life of a practitioner. Each reflection is also accompanied by three Guided Inquiry Questions and an Exploration question or activity.

Do yourself a favor and date each entry you make on a page. In time, these dates and thoughts will record a journey of development that you will want to review and cherish as you seek to develop the next generation of practitioners. Be honest, be open, be yourself, understand yourself, push yourself, develop others, and be the practitioner entities need and people deserve.

Reflection

I do not want the world to only study a method . . . I want them to find its end, push its boundaries, and make it anew.

Personal Reactions

Agree? Disagree? Seen examples? How would you use this? Date entries, revisit from time to time—sketch if useful!

Guided Inquiry

1. If your career was a book, what would your introduction say? Write it.

2. How can change management demand improvement without improving itself? Or is there value in stability?

3. Who are you going to talk to about this reflection?

Exploration

Find a process improvement tool, and modify it to add functionality, usability, etc. Then, test it during a project or other initiative.

No. 1

Title

I am a Sensei. I am a Shihan. I am a Leader. I am an Executive.

These are false.

Once you set aside the title 'student', you become lost.

Personal Reactions

Agree? Disagree? Seen examples? How would you use this? Date entries, revisit from time to time—sketch if useful!

DOI: 10.4324/9781003507383-1

Guided Inquiry

1. How do you engage in continuous learning in your current position?

2. Have you used continuous learning to prepare for your next role?

3. How do you handle someone using a title to avoid growth and development?

Exploration

Become a student again if you haven't been one for a while. If you have, expand your scope. Seek out a learning opportunity, work related or not, and dig in!

Tool: Your Library

As every student accesses a library, so must the practitioner. It is imperative that someone involved in change management establish and maintain a library of materials, hardcopy and/or digital, throughout their career, even if they leave change management. Remember, you may leave a position tasked with direct change management or operational excellence, but you will NEVER leave a role that engages change, no matter where you go or what you do.

There are no rules in forming and curating this library. If it helps you manage changes and the elements thereof (teams, budgets, project management, mentoring/coaching, career development, etc.), include it. Make sure your library is accessible and is in your primary work space. Also, make a wish list of books and items for your library so that when birthdays and holidays come along, you know what you want!

If you don't already have a shelf started for your library, let's get this going. Make a list below of the books and items you need to collect, and get those items situated in your work space.

DOI: 10.4324/9781003507383-2

Item	**Current Location**	**Moved**

No. 2

Purpose

When you are gone, what will the world know of you?

Will they study that you existed? That is laudable.

Will they study what you left behind? That is knowledge.

Will they advance beyond what you left behind? This is impact.

Personal Reactions

Agree? Disagree? Seen examples? How would you use this? Date entries, revisit from time to time—sketch if useful!

DOI: 10.4324/9781003507383-3

Guided Inquiry

1. How do you personally define legacy?

2. What forces (personal, professional, or both) have impacted that definition?

3. Upon reflection, do you need to modify your definition? Why or why not?

Exploration

Find examples of people, well known or not, that fit each clause of the reflection. Why do they fit this clause and not another? Did something limit them? Did something push them?

No. 3

Pursuit

Building toward a goal or outcome is total—all encompassing.

Meaning like the sea, it surrounds.

It ebbs and flows, never stopping.

Personal Reactions

Agree? Disagree? Seen examples? How would you use this? Date entries, revisit from time to time—sketch if useful!

DOI: 10.4324/9781003507383-4

Guided Inquiry

1. What stopped you from achieving a goal in the past?

2. Explore a time when you just stopped caring about a project or goal. Why?

3. Do your goals build on previous goals? How? If so or if not, why?

Exploration

Take a current goal or write a new one. Now, build on it. What goal comes next? Then, what goals comes after that? Create a flow of goals for the next 3 years.

No. 4

Opportunity

The practitioner is needed wherever he or she finds his or herself.

Personal Reactions

Agree? Disagree? Seen examples? How would you use this? Date entries, revisit from time to time—sketch if useful!

DOI: 10.4324/9781003507383-5

Guided Inquiry

1. Explore a project you were assigned but didn't want. How did it turn out?

____

____

2. Have you ever benefited by completing a project/task no one else wanted?

____

____

3. How do you, or should you, decide what your next project will be?

____

____

Exploration

Go out into the world. Sit in a space like a restaurant, department store, or some other space where stuff is happening. What situations do you see crying out for a change agent and improvement? Why?

____

____

____

____

____

____

____

No. 5

Self-Importance

If you underestimate the value of an engagement or task, you have overestimated your own value as well.

Personal Reactions

Agree? Disagree? Seen examples? How would you use this? Date entries, revisit from time to time—sketch if useful!

DOI: 10.4324/9781003507383-6

Guided Inquiry

1. When have you received an assignment that you felt was below you?

___

___

2. How did you cope with this feeling? Did it pass? What did you do?

___

___

3. How have you dealt with people who were self-important?

___

___

Exploration

How do you define the value you bring to a project or entity? If you had five simple sentences to explain this, like an elevator pitch, what would you say?

___

___

___

___

___

___

___

Tool: Quote Archive

It seems kind of antiquated, but having a collection of quotes that address different facets and issues of change management can be helpful in both focusing your action and thoughts, but can also be instructive to those facing and/or facilitating change. A quote on hard work can make the team see the value of its efforts. A quote on developing a skill can help someone gain the courage to undertake professional development. This book's dedication held two quotes from Theodore Roosevelt on work and the hurdles faced when seeking to make things better. Here are few more of my favorites:

> Do what you can, with what you have, where you are.
>
> **Theodore Roosevelt**

> Yesterday is not ours to recover, but tomorrow is ours to win or to lose. I am resolved that we shall win the tomorrows before us.
>
> **Lyndon Johnson**

> I will not follow where the path may lead, but I will go where there is no path, and I will leave a trail.
>
> **Muriel Strode**

DOI: 10.4324/9781003507383-7

> Be extremely subtle, even to the point of formlessness. Be extremely mysterious, even to the point of soundlessness. Thereby you can be the director of the opponent's fate.
>
> **Sun Tzu**

> It turns out that facts may not really be facts; they can change as the verification changes; they may only tell part of the story, not the whole story; or they may be so qualified by verifiers that they're empty of information.
>
> **Colin Powell**

> When your values are clear to you, making decisions becomes easier.
>
> **Roy Disney**

Keep a notebook or other record of quotes and their subjects. Use them as meeting openers, tone-setting devices, or just simple anchor points to show others have experienced the same issues we live with today.

No. 6

Perspective

If you are the only answer to a problem, you have misread the question.

Personal Reactions

Agree? Disagree? Seen examples? How would you use this? Date entries, revisit from time to time—sketch if useful!

DOI: 10.4324/9781003507383-8

Guided Inquiry

1. How do you build a team to tackle a project?

____

____

2. Explore a time when you failed to ask for help and what happened.

____

____

3. Are there situations wherein pretending you know everything is beneficial?

____

____

Exploration

List out your top 5–7 career skills. Next to these, write the names of others you know and/or work with who have the same mastery of that skill that you do. Next to them, write another name. Does this dilute the value of your skill? Could it show bench strength for your organization? Could this tell you the skills you need in a new hire? How can this help you manage team talent?

____

____

____

____

____

No. 7

Role

The practitioner advocates for all but him or herself.

Personal Reactions

Agree? Disagree? Seen examples? How would you use this? Date entries, revisit from time to time—sketch if useful!

DOI: 10.4324/9781003507383-9

Guided Inquiry

1. We have all done it. Explain a time when you advocated for yourself.

____

____

2. When have you advocated for someone else? What happened?

____

____

3. What does 'advocacy' mean to you?

____

____

Exploration

Could you be better in using advocacy to meet goals, project outcomes, or build team morale? List 3–5 things you can do immediately to prioritize advocacy.

____

____

____

____

____

____

____

____

No. 8

Duty

If you find yourself ready to remove a project team member, know that you are the one needing to go.

Personal Reactions

Agree? Disagree? Seen examples? How would you use this? Date entries, revisit from time to time—sketch if useful!

DOI: 10.4324/9781003507383-10

Guided Inquiry

1. Have you ever removed someone from a team? How did it work out?

____

____

2. How do you deal with problematic team members?

____

____

3. Have you ever removed yourself from a project team? Explain.

____

____

Exploration

What are your top skills in addressing a team member you have decided is problematic? What new skills would be helpful? Select 1–2 of these new skills and find training options to add them to your toolbox.

____

____

____

____

____

____

____

____

No. 9

Perception

If a practitioner has enemies, he/she also has opportunities.

Personal Reactions

Agree? Disagree? Seen examples? How would you use this? Date entries, revisit from time to time—sketch if useful!

DOI: 10.4324/9781003507383-11

Guided Inquiry

1. How have you made someone an enemy?

2. Have you ever converted an enemy to be an ally? Explain.

3. How can someone be an enemy of a project and yet an ally elsewhere?

Exploration

Explore the life of a role model or hero. How did they handle enemies and allies? Could they work with both? How does their approach impact you and any future skill development?

No. 10

Pretense

The story told to brag is the rotten board on a high bridge.

Whereas a story told to teach or, better yet, to fuel further thought, is a strong stone from which one builds a lasting span.

Personal Reactions

Agree? Disagree? Seen examples? How would you use this? Date entries, revisit from time to time—sketch if useful!

DOI: 10.4324/9781003507383-12

Guided Inquiry

1. Explore a time when you were impacted by someone bragging.

____

____

2. When have you participated in a lessons-learned activity on a project?

____

____

3. Is bragging inherently negative?

____

____

Exploration

Time to do some research. Look for stories where results were touted AND inflated. What happened?

____

____

____

____

____

____

____

____

No. 11

Work

Mastery exhibited in words is a sculpture of mist and fog.

Personal Reactions

Agree? Disagree? Seen examples? How would you use this? Date entries, revisit from time to time—sketch if useful!

DOI: 10.4324/9781003507383-13

Guided Inquiry

1. If you listed your top five skills, how would you prove you have that skill?

____

____

2. Can you master a skill without actually using it? Think practice vs. use.

____

____

3. What proof, if any, do you look for in others as proof of their skillset?

____

____

Exploration

Think back on a project occurring during the last 2–3 years. Was there a situation wherein someone failed to perform at their self-proclaimed proficiency level? What happened? Did you have to take any mitigating actions?

____

____

____

____

____

____

No. 12

Obstacle

If the practitioner has found an obstacle, they have found themselves.

Personal Reactions

Agree? Disagree? Seen examples? How would you use this? Date entries, revisit from time to time—sketch if useful!

DOI: 10.4324/9781003507383-14

Guided Inquiry

1. How can a change agent be an obstacle to progress and/or success?

____

____

2. What do you do when you find you are at the limit of your abilities?

____

____

3. How do you address obstacles encountered during projects and initiatives?

____

____

Exploration

Imagine you are running a change practitioner training program. How would you go about training the students to recognize the cause of obstacles and their resolution? How would you teach them to understand when they may be the obstacle?

____

____

____

____

____

____

____

Tool: Know Your Path

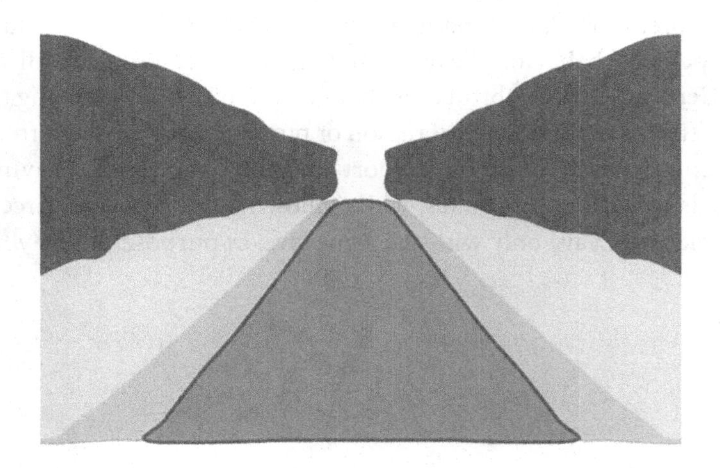

Visualizing, even abstractly, one's purpose and mission can be a powerful approach to staying on target, evaluating opportunities that arise, and achieving your vision of personal and professional success. I have often directed employees, teammates, mentees, and even mentors to visualize a path. I bring to mind a wide path of concrete or rock that is edged by short grass that after a few yards' transitions to tall, prairie grass before merging into the woods. Next, I tell them the path is their career, their private life, their existence. Everything they do is done to make progress on the path. We must be diligent in staying on the path and avoiding the pitfalls of the tall grass and woods.

DOI: 10.4324/9781003507383-15

That path offers a way to focus. Is the offered new job on your path? Is making a new product on your path? Is getting involved in a coworker spat on your path? Is criticizing a decision from management at the coffee pot on your path? Finding whether or not something is on your path is powerful because, quietly simply, it tells you where you belong and where you do not. Staying on the path takes focus and purpose. If I stray, is it a stumble or am I veering off to build a new path which I will follow with the same purposefulness? Or am I wildly hacking through the tall grass and have no idea where I am or why I'm headed this direction?

The path also affords protection. Efforts driving and leading change are fraught with distractions, subterfuge, resistance, and losses. If I have an employee who is path focused, I can give them top cover. If they are out in the tall grass or into the trees, they are off mission and I have lost sight of them and could be powerless to help. An example I often use to illustrate this is any movie where a group awaits the attack from an enemy. Often, someone breaks rank and meets a hasty demise. What was the purpose of that person's behavior? Fear? Panic? Impatience? Probably all of the above. Certainly, it is doubtful they thought a solo charge was going to win the day. That said, for no logical reason or purpose, they deviated from the plan, stepped away from their support structure, and failed. Leaving the path leads to terminal mistakes, while following it focuses resources and guides success. Leave only with the same level of purposefulness you had while on it.

No. 13

Achievement

Recounting the deeds of the past is entertainment, not a credential or a placeholder for absent results.

Personal Reactions

Agree? Disagree? Seen examples? How would you use this? Date entries, revisit from time to time—sketch if useful!

DOI: 10.4324/9781003507383-16

Guided Inquiry

1. When is there value in recounting past successes?

2. What kind of results matter in determining project success?

3. Can you ever outperform the need to have positive results?

Exploration

Have you ever worked with someone who sat on past successes? How did they do this? How was it perceived and/or tolerated?

No. 14

Reward

How does one get credit for solving the complex and advancing the organization?

By getting to take on the next assignment.

Credit is for those who plan never to achieve again.

Personal Reactions

Agree? Disagree? Seen examples? How would you use this? Date entries, revisit from time to time—sketch if useful!

DOI: 10.4324/9781003507383-17

Guided Inquiry

1. What do you consider a reward?

2. How do you use your successes in your career?

3. Explore how success in one role can prevent advancement to other roles.

Exploration

Watch a movie or series of movies with a clear hero or super hero. Is there a point wherein being called on becomes a burden? If so, when does this occur? Is it solvable? How?

No. 15

Humility

Pursuing something to make yourself feel superior over another is not a meaningful or fulfilling journey.

Personal Reactions

Agree? Disagree? Seen examples? How would you use this? Date entries, revisit from time to time—sketch if useful!

DOI: 10.4324/9781003507383-18

Guided Inquiry

1. Has a possession ever made you feel superior to another person? Explain.

2. How do you check your motives in pursuing a project or initiative?

3. What motivates someone to hold feelings of superiority?

Exploration

It is time to volunteer. If you do so already, add a few hours. If you don't, get started. Find something that interests you, but most importantly, actively engage in making a difference.

No. 16

Versatility

Three persons each dig. One digs with a spade, another with a trowel, and the last with hands. And what do we have? Three holes.

Personal Reactions

Agree? Disagree? Seen examples? How would you use this? Date entries, revisit from time to time—sketch if useful!

DOI: 10.4324/9781003507383-19

Guided Inquiry

1. Are diversity of approach and methods valuable? Explain.

___

___

2. How do available resources dictate the methods used to solve a problem?

___

___

3. How do you select the best tools and approach for a project?

___

___

Exploration

Pick a recurring task, either at work or at home. List 2–3 different ways to achieve the desired end result. Now, use each one and assess if there were any differences. Was one faster? Slower? More fun? More cumbersome? What attributes were important in determining the best approach?

___

___

___

___

___

___

___

Tool: Pocket Cards

Standard 3×5 index cards, ruled or unruled, are incredibly versatile tools for the change agent. Cards easily fit in a shirt or pants pocket and can hold a litany of information. Pre-printed cards can be handed out to team members and colleagues. Referencing a card can be done almost covertly and if done overtly is perceived as being less dismissive than looking at a smartphone. Further, the card does not have banners and notifications like your phone screen, which can be distracting and take your attention away from looking for the information you needed. If cards aren't your style, a small pocket notebook is just as useful and provides space to take additional notes.

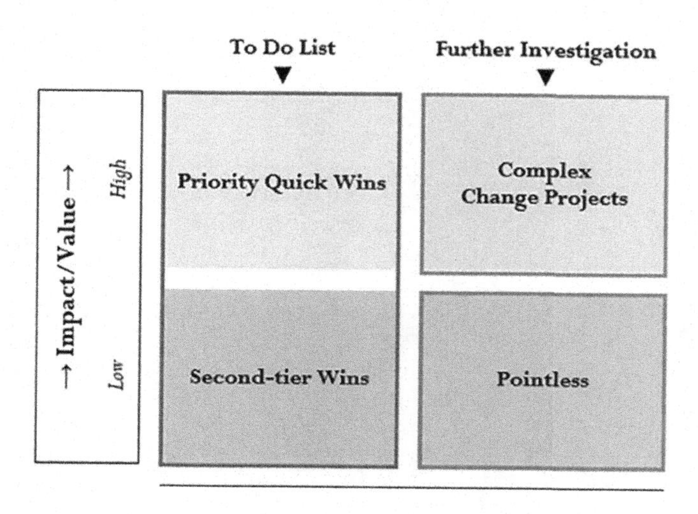

DOI: 10.4324/9781003507383-20

No. 17

Diplomacy

Exercise caution with what you sow.

You may grow thorns instead of food.

Personal Reactions

Agree? Disagree? Seen examples? How would you use this? Date entries, revisit from time to time—sketch if useful!

DOI: 10.4324/9781003507383-21

Guided Inquiry

1. How do you define ‘diplomacy’?

2. Does using diplomacy always avoid negative repercussions? Explain.

3. Is it ever productive to be authoritarian? What are the ramifications?

Exploration

Have you ever seen someone ‘poison the well’? Why did they do it? What were the outcomes?

No. 18

Flexibility

Pursue with fluidity, but with purposefulness.

There are a thousand paths to any destination.

Ask yourself, what is more important: Getting there or how we got there?

The answers do not overlap.

Personal Reactions

Agree? Disagree? Seen examples? How would you use this? Date entries, revisit from time to time—sketch if useful!

DOI: 10.4324/9781003507383-22

Guided Inquiry

1. How do you avoid getting sidetracked in a project or initiative?

2. It may be cliché, but do the end results ever justify the means used?

3. What matters more: the change methodology used or the result? Why?

Exploration

How can flexibility of approach be used to manage resources, staffing, and outcomes? How about flexibility's influence on professional development?

No. 19

Agility

Your everyday carry should not include decades of baggage.

Carry the useful and jettison the dead weight.

Freedom is empowering, and agility is transcendent.

Personal Reactions

Agree? Disagree? Seen examples? How would you use this? Date entries, revisit from time to time—sketch if useful!

DOI: 10.4324/9781003507383-23

Guided Inquiry

1. Why do some hold on to the past at the cost of the future?

____

____

2. How do you break the ‘this is how we’ve always done it’ obstacle?

____

____

3. What do you do if the baggage was bad process improvement?

____

____

Exploration

What is the value of emotional freedom and agile thought in change management?

____

____

____

____

____

____

____

____

____

No. 20

Nurture

Innovation and change start with a simple practice: reward curiosity.

Personal Reactions

Agree? Disagree? Seen examples? How would you use this? Date entries, revisit from time to time—sketch if useful!

DOI: 10.4324/9781003507383-24

Guided Inquiry

1. Is curiosity rewarded where you work? How?

2. How can curiosity be leveraged as a source of change management projects?

3. Have you seen or experienced situations in which curiosity was stifled?

Exploration

Buy a simple pocket notebook or use this book (skip the phone app for notes, once you open your phone, you'll get distracted). For 3–4 weeks, keep a running list of anything and everything that sparks curiosity. After this period, go back and see if anything might be the start of a process improvement or other project. Challenge others to do the same or create an idea board at work where colleagues can write a simple sticky note and post an idea for review. Reward implemented ideas.

No. 21

Intentionality

It is critical to know if one is chasing a goal or running away from a problem.

Personal Reactions

Agree? Disagree? Seen examples? How would you use this? Date entries, revisit from time to time—sketch if useful!

DOI: 10.4324/9781003507383-25

Guided Inquiry

1. When was the last time you completely replaced a goal with a new measure?

____

____

2. Do your goals focus on your strengths? Is this useful? What are you missing?

____

____

3. How do you know your goals are impactful?

____

____

Exploration

Think about an operational or performance issue at work. How can you craft a goal to address and resolve it? Should goals be about measuring our successes or our improvements?

____

____

____

____

____

____

Tool: Impact Matrix

Yes, it is simple and one of the basic tools of process improvement, but in its simplicity is a useful amount of versatility. While referred to with titles that are a mixture of the words Action, Priority, Impact, and Effort in various parings, what I was taught as the Impact Matrix is a simple tool that allows a quick analysis of resources needed compared to value achieved. This tool is great for finding quick wins to build momentum for a team, program, or initiative. It is a great tool for vetting project ideas and understanding that not all change management is a resource heavy endeavor … sometimes a quick, simple adjustment can be epic in impact and cost very little to execute.

DOI: 10.4324/9781003507383-26

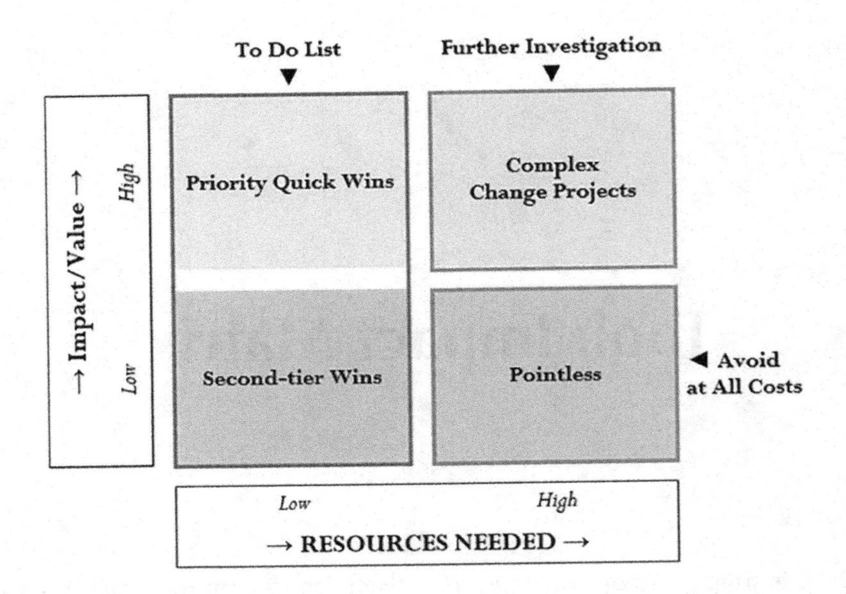
To Do List
Further Investigation
→ Impact/Value →
High
Low
Priority Quick Wins
Complex
Change Projects
Second-tier Wins
Pointless
Avoid
at All Costs
Low
High
→ RESOURCES NEEDED →

No. 22

Hypotheticals

Asking practice questions is avoiding learning actual lessons.

Personal Reactions

Agree? Disagree? Seen examples? How would you use this? Date entries, revisit from time to time—sketch if useful!

DOI: 10.4324/9781003507383-27

Guided Inquiry

1. Do you find hypotheticals useful?

2. Why would an entity value using hypotheticals?

3. Can hypotheticals be as impactful as actual work that yields real experience?

Exploration

Review your favorite sources of news and information and find some examples of hypotheticals. Were they used well? Could they have been better? Would a different approach have been more instructive?

No. 23

Progress

Re-living past actions is a false substitute for progress.

Personal Reactions

Agree? Disagree? Seen examples? How would you use this? Date entries, revisit from time to time—sketch if useful!

DOI: 10.4324/9781003507383-28

Guided Inquiry

1. Have you ever worked somewhere stuck in its past successes?

   ____

   ____

2. What does 'progress' look like for an organization? Who defines/measures it?

   ____

   ____

3. Have you ever worked with someone who is too tied to their past success?

   ____

   ____

Exploration

Look at the goals you have for yourself, team, or entity. Are they based on what is achievable? Is this progress? Draft 3–5 new goals that measure new progress and not simple advancement within a metric. For example, if you handle improvement projects for the factory floor, would it be helpful to shift to the shipping department?

____

____

____

____

____

No. 24

Scope

When you have proceduralized the insignificant, only the true problems remain unsolved.

Personal Reactions

Agree? Disagree? Seen examples? How would you use this? Date entries, revisit from time to time—sketch if useful!

DOI: 10.4324/9781003507383-29

Guided Inquiry

1. How do you determine what is worth improving?

____

____

2. How have you seen leaders avoid the conflict of change?

____

____

3. What is the longest period of time you've seen a serious problem ignored?

____

____

Exploration

Take out a workplace manual, guide, policies, or other collection of documents. Chart out what part of your operations are covered. Once done, review the list. Are these the most stable, problem-free segments of your operations? What areas are missing or under-represented? Why? Are these areas stable? Does this help you understand where to allocate your time?

____

____

____

____

____

____

Tool: Envision Your Customer

Successful and enduring process improvement and change management cannot happen without first identifying and knowing your customer.

This may seem simple, but notice what was said: identifying AND knowing your customer. This is not simply having a customer, defining them, and perhaps speaking with one or two. No, this means seeing the world through their eyes and assessing what you are doing from their perspectives. Change initiatives launch all the time with only a basic idea of who the customer is and less than zero understanding of them. I have seen project teams focus on a new system to such an extent that they never envisioned a helpline and email would be needed because the solution's customers were people who would, at some point, have questions.

Thankfully, the change agent or operational excellence practitioner does not have to invent a method for gaining this focus and understanding of the customer. Practitioners in design thinking and innovation processes based on this practice have created the tools you will need. The core tool of this effort is the empathy map, a one-page document that forces you to collect what a customer sees, hears, thinks, feels, says, and does. This in turn gives you a worldview from which you can find what their real problems are, what they value, and how you can develop a solution that will be useful and impactful to them. A simple Google search for 'empathy map' will give you several examples. Further, books like *Business Model Generation: A Handbook for Visionaries, Game Changers, and Challengers*

DOI: 10.4324/9781003507383-30

by Alexander Osterwalder and Yves Pigneur (John Wiley and Sons, 2010) provide excellent empathy maps and discussion on how to use them.

Also understand that classic Lean and Lean Six Sigma tools like process walks and stakeholder interviews give you the information needed to complete the empathy map.

While such a map is ideally made during the beginning stages of an engagement, it is not meant to be a stagnant tool. Rather, periodically check it at major decision points to make sure your work aligns with your customer and make modifications should your understanding or perspective on the customer change as you learn more. This alignment can and should be further scrutinized during testing of proposed solutions before final implementation.

No. 25

Resurrect

Why it did not happen is not as important as what can make it happen now.

Personal Reactions

Agree? Disagree? Seen examples? How would you use this? Date entries, revisit from time to time—sketch if useful!

DOI: 10.4324/9781003507383-31

Guided Inquiry

1. Explore a time when you missed a deadline and the opportunity that was lost.

    ____

    ____

2. Have you ever resurrected a missed opportunity or dead project? Explain.

    ____

    ____

3. How do you rebuild trust, with leadership, team, and yourself, after failing?

    ____

    ____

Exploration

List 2–3 opportunities missed or failed projects. Are any worthy and capable of being resurrected? If so, how? Develop a plan and write a one-pager on how to make it work.

____

____

____

____

____

____

No. 26

Increments

If you are saying 'No', can you provide any form or element of a 'Yes'?

Personal Reactions

Agree? Disagree? Seen examples? How would you use this? Date entries, revisit from time to time—sketch if useful!

DOI: 10.4324/9781003507383-32

Guided Inquiry

1. Are their people/teams in your organization who have a rep for saying 'no'?

____

____

2. How would you or do you go about assessing what is doable in a request?

____

____

3. How can saying 'no' be temporary? Can 'no' change to 'yes' based on timing?

____

____

Exploration

Explore the last few times when you have denied a request (doesn't matter what it was for). Why did you deny it? If pieced out, could some elements have been doable? Any regrets on the decisions you made?

____

____

____

____

____

____

No. 27

Value

No problem has a magic combination that renders it moot if one complains enough.

Puzzles are solved by a sharp mind, not a sharp or overly productive tongue.

Personal Reactions

Agree? Disagree? Seen examples? How would you use this? Date entries, revisit from time to time—sketch if useful!

DOI: 10.4324/9781003507383-33

Guided Inquiry

1. How do you deal with people who only complain and never take action?

____

____

2. Ever dealt with a 'funny guy' who loves quips or insults and avoids work?

____

____

3. Do you have a favored approach to tackling problems? Has it been successful?

____

____

Exploration

Write out your standard approach to assessing a problem or operational issue. Now, edit. Simplify it. Cut unneeded words. Could images help? Next, find a few 3×5 notecards (ruled or unruled). Reduce your methodology to the notecard. Could this be given to another person as a cheat sheet? If so, why not give it to your team?

____

____

____

____

____

No. 28

Dissent

The practitioner must listen deeply for the chirp of the quietest bird for often it warns of the arrival of the most dangerous of storms.

Personal Reactions

Agree? Disagree? Seen examples? How would you use this? Date entries, revisit from time to time—sketch if useful!

DOI: 10.4324/9781003507383-34

Guided Inquiry

1. Have you ever worked with a quiet yet highly observant person? Explain.

____

____

2. What are the major roadblocks employees face in raising issues with leaders?

____

____

3. When is dissent helpful? How do we assess its value? When is it an issue?

____

____

Exploration

Explore an example, either from your career or from a story found elsewhere, of a seemingly small issue that quickly grew into a transformative problem. How was it missed or ignored? How did it grow? Was it solvable or was it terminal? What would you have done differently?

____

____

____

____

____

Tool: Grief and Change

As you well know, change is difficult for any number of reasons whether it involves time, money, other resources, or just being able to crack the code on a problem. That said, change is even more complicated than that, especially when human emotions are considered.

In many projects I have either worked or supervised, one reaction was often, though not always, encountered: grief. While team members, leaders, and those who simply know a project is going on will be subject to feelings of fear, anxiety, sadness, excitement, and worry, to name a few, those closest to the changed process or processes will likely also experience grief. Consider this, if for the last 15 years you showed up at work everyday and used the same process each day to do your work, that process takes on an identity of sorts that can be as emotionally real and significant as a human coworker. If the process user is part of the change team—as they most likely will be—they will likely see actions taken against that process. As the process is described, explored, and edited or replaced, the former user is there to experience it all.

As a change agent, you must be cognizant that team members may go through the five stages of grieving: denial, anger, bargaining, depression, and acceptance. Understand that this is about the process effectively passing away. They may also experience grief separately if duties, locations, offices, and coworkers change.

DOI: 10.4324/9781003507383-35

It is easy when projects are driven by metrics and analyses to forget that the work being done is done by humans who experience emotions with almost any circumstance. Just as understanding our customer is critical to making meaningful change, we must also understand the humanity inside the entities we serve that are impacted by our work. You will need to be sensitive, be supportive, and help all through their times of need. It is recommended that you do some reading on grief and grief support and be able to extrapolate these learnings to your project teams as needed.

No. 29

Simplicity

Never doubt how mesmerizing and powerful the obvious can be.

Personal Reactions

Agree? Disagree? Seen examples? How would you use this? Date entries, revisit from time to time—sketch if useful!

DOI: 10.4324/9781003507383-36

Guided Inquiry

1. Give an example of a time when someone tried to over-complicate a solution.

   ____

   ____

2. Why are simple and obvious solutions often overlooked or distrusted?

   ____

   ____

3. How can you capitalize on impactful simple solutions to drive change?

   ____

   ____

Exploration

Time to pick some fruit—low-hanging fruit. Consider a problematic process, team, or product. Make a list of changes and then using an impact matrix, find 2–4 easy wins (anything with low effort, prioritize high impact, but low impact is fine as well). If you did these actions, how would teams and the entity react? Could this be used to build change momentum? Give it a shot.

____

____

____

____

____

No. 30

Weaponization

The practitioner is not a weapon, and any attempt to make him or her one is a failure on many fronts.

Personal Reactions

Agree? Disagree? Seen examples? How would you use this? Date entries, revisit from time to time—sketch if useful!

DOI: 10.4324/9781003507383-37

Guided Inquiry

1. What do you do when your entity wants to use change efforts punitively?

____

____

2. As a change agent, have you ever been used as an enforcer? Explain.

____

____

3. How do you make needed management changes and not appear punitive?

____

____

Exploration

It will happen sooner or later if it hasn't already—so let's prepare. Assume you are being sent to make some needed changes in both management and processes in a team. It's clear, some want this to be punitive. Develop 3–5 strategies to avoid appearing punitive and the situations in which these approaches are most effective. The key is to mitigate the perception of punishment.

____

____

____

____

No. 31

Favoritism

Advocating differentially based on personal need will soon leave you with no one to advance at all.

Personal Reactions

Agree? Disagree? Seen examples? How would you use this? Date entries, revisit from time to time—sketch if useful!

DOI: 10.4324/9781003507383-38

Guided Inquiry

1. How do you strategically advance individuals without alienating the team?

___

___

2. How do you explain why some are promoted or favored and others are not?

___

___

3. Have you seen a leader use advancement as a weapon against team members?

___

___

Exploration

Explore the reasoning you use in choosing to mentor someone or participate either actively or passively in advancing their development and career. Are you focused on them? Yourself? Solving a short- or long-term issue? Explore your motives and how these may be perceived. Do you need to do any perception management?

___

___

___

___

No. 32

Drive

Each protest against success helps others build a path to excellence.

Personal Reactions

Agree? Disagree? Seen examples? How would you use this? Date entries, revisit from time to time—sketch if useful!

DOI: 10.4324/9781003507383-39

Guided Inquiry

1. How do you assess the motives of and deal with the naysayers on a team?

2. How do you support those wanting change when they face those who don't?

3. How do you handle naysayers when they are members of leadership?

Exploration

Find a case study in history wherein a group succeeded in obtaining an objective despite significant negatively, doubt, and protests. How did they handle the negativity? Did those solutions last or require pivots? Was success lasting? Would you have done anything differently?

No. 33

Resources

If I give you my best rocks or steel, won't you be able to build the best bridge?

Personal Reactions

Agree? Disagree? Seen examples? How would you use this? Date entries, revisit from time to time—sketch if useful!

DOI: 10.4324/9781003507383-40

Guided Inquiry

1. When were you not given what you needed for a project? How'd you cope?

2. Are the outcomes built with limited resources actually flawed?

3. How do you advocate for the resources you need for a project or initiative?

Exploration

Look back at a project or decision wherein you had limited resources. Explore the results and consider what would have happened if you had been given all that you requested. Were these missing assets actually needed? Explain.

Tool: Force Fields

Yes, another simple tool. But like the Impact Matrix, Force Field Analysis can give you a quick, easy, and visual way to analyze the forces at play on a goal, outcome, or range of other deliverables. There are several different ways to do an FFA, so if the below does not quite fit your situation, hit the Internet and look for another design. I favor the below method because it can be taught in minutes and drawn on anything from a napkin to a whiteboard. While traditionally the forces restraining or driving are doing so on a specific goal or outcome, I like to sometimes use a range or degrees of success. This allows us to see if we lack key resources and supports because while we have enough driving forces to succeed, our success will be limited.

DOI: 10.4324/9781003507383-41

Example: We have three options: maintain, upgrade, or replace a system. A limiting factor is money, so that blocks a new system. However, the system is unstable in its current state, so maintaining is not possible and we have enough money for an upgrade.

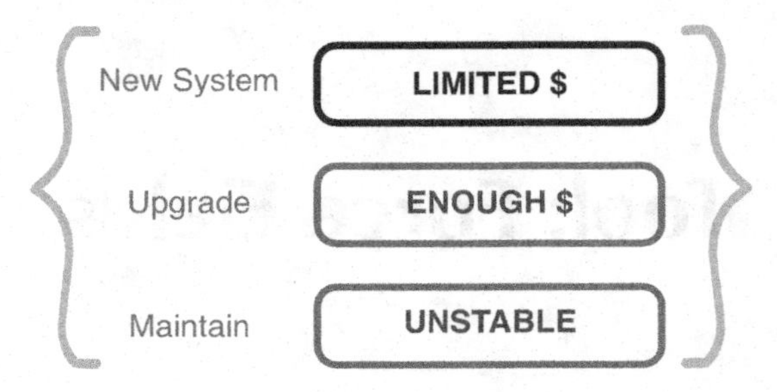

Using the FFA to understand levels of success is an effective way to illustrate what you can do in response to a problem. Even when using a more traditional FFA format, you can easily see the constraints needing to be addressed and develop a mitigation plan. Again, while simple, the FFA is immensely powerful.

No. 34

Conservation

If we constantly plant and pull, plant and pull, we will exhaust our ground.

Be mindful of your resources.

Personal Reactions

Agree? Disagree? Seen examples? How would you use this? Date entries, revisit from time to time—sketch if useful!

DOI: 10.4324/9781003507383-42

Guided Inquiry

1. Have you ever called on one team member or asset too much? Explain.

____

____

2. How do you avoid over-taxing project resources with special requests?

____

____

3. How do you avoid change burn out with functional areas at work?

____

____

Exploration

Farmers rotate crops to make sure their fields stay fertile and are not overburdened. Looking at either yourself or a team of change agents you might lead, how do you rotate work assignments to keep them fresh? Can they work in different areas? Handle different types of projects? Or do you allow rotation at all? If you don't might it be a strategy you'd like to explore implementing?

____

____

____

____

____

No. 35

Success

Easily choosing success is opting to fail.

Success is built, not chosen.

Personal Reactions

Agree? Disagree? Seen examples? How would you use this? Date entries, revisit from time to time—sketch if useful!

DOI: 10.4324/9781003507383-43

Guided Inquiry

1. How do you define 'success' for a change management effort or project?

2. Explore a time when a project was cut-short to realize a quick win.

3. How do you build change management success? Team? Resources? Projects?

Exploration

Previously, we've discussed the value of easy wins in a larger scope of change management that also includes complex projects. Looking back on projects and initiatives you've been involved in, could a change management program focus solely on easy wins and still be 'successful'? Is success more valuable if it is complicated to attain?

No. 36

Unity

There is immense power in a team. Build connections. Form a square and address challenges. Fight shoulder to shoulder.

But know this, the further you get away from the team, the more perilous your situation.

Understand that distance is the first step in defeat.

Personal Reactions

Agree? Disagree? Seen examples? How would you use this? Date entries, revisit from time to time—sketch if useful!

DOI: 10.4324/9781003507383-44

Guided Inquiry

1. How do you handle someone that is breaking from the team? Does it work?

___

___

2. Explore a time when a team you were a part of or led fell apart. Causes?

___

___

3. What do you look for in building a team? Why?

___

___

Exploration

In reviewing the reflection above, re-read the tool 'Know Your Path'. How do you build a team and stick with it? More importantly, how do you build a vision and stick with it, both as a leader and a professional? Are you successful in keeping the team on mission? Are you successful in keeping your career on mission? If not, what do you need to change? How?

___

___

___

___

___

Tool: Team-Centered Leadership

No matter what you call it, whether it is process improvement, change management, quality improvement, or some mixture thereof, making meaningful change that lasts is a team sport. And for that team, it is a contact sport.

There is a strong vortex where team and leadership meet, as they are inextricably linked concepts. Few efforts undertaken in operations are solo ventures. We are always part of a team whether we know it or not. Teams involve people. Therefore, human behavior drives the team and its work, and this requires leadership. Not bossing, but leadership.

Using the logic of the empathy map common in product design and development as a structure, these core concepts form a basis for empathetic leadership that will build an unstoppable team and supportive leadership culture.

Think

People Feel Before They Know. A team won't work if the members don't feel valued. People will share information to make themselves

DOI: 10.4324/9781003507383-45

look important. People share their efforts when they care about the result and the team.

Understanding. Everyone is different. Motivations are different. Actions and methods are different. Seek to understand the teammate and what is happening, good or bad.

Accessibility. Chains of command devalue the team. Members of management all the way to the CEO should be approachable and open to anyone raising issue or presenting an idea. This builds an environment of safety and security, and makes the teammates feel valued. I take action on items brought to me every day.

Feel

Responsibility. As a leader, you are responsible for everything a team does. Own the mistakes, and highlight the successes. You own the issues, and they own the success.

Defense. Welcome criticism and feedback. Don't welcome blame, fault-finding, or attack. Shield your team.

Let Things Go. You can't get very far carrying yesterday, the day before, last week, last year, or last decade with you. Dump the baggage. Let things go.

Say

Identity. Share the Mission and Vision you have for the endeavor, whether it is a project or an entire agency. Further, establish core beliefs that support the Mission and Vision.

Empowerment. Know when to get out of the way. You have teammates and teams for a reason. Give them what they need, support and defend, but most importantly, set them loose!

Growth. Know what teammates want out of their current position and out of their careers. Help them get there through coaching and developmental opportunities. Support growth, even if it means they leave your agency.

Do

Honesty. With good news and bad. Be fair, be clear, be understanding, and be honest. They may not like what you say, but they will appreciate that you said it. Honesty shows that you value the teammate. Show it.

Listen. Absolutely critical. You're not promising to agree, but you are promising to hear them out.

Teach—Don't Command. Even if you want them to do something else, don't give an order unless absolutely necessary. Rather, help them reason through the issue. Maybe they see something you don't? Maybe you see something they don't? They need to flex the mental and emotional muscles. If you command each time, you'll be making endless decisions. If you teach them through it, it lessens your workload and it helps them grow as a leader.

Lead by Example. No duty is below you. Leading by example shows the team what is real. No task is below me, and I do not allow others to think tasks are below them.

No. 37

Strength

Nothing that lasts is based upon criticizing the few.

Instead, find the unbreakable strength in the acceptance of many.

Personal Reactions

Agree? Disagree? Seen examples? How would you use this? Date entries, revisit from time to time—sketch if useful!

DOI: 10.4324/9781003507383-46

Guided Inquiry

1. Explore a time when, despite leadership buy-in, staff distrusted a project.

   ___

   ___

2. How do you make changes without criticizing those responsible for an issue?

   ___

   ___

3. What are your top 3–5 strategies to get change buy-in from staff and leaders?

   ___

   ___

Exploration

Explore a project, either in your career or in something you have encountered in a book or news article wherein it appeared criticism and critique were more important to the key players than resolution of the underlying issue(s). Why do you think this was the case? Did it change? What would you have done differently? Have you ever been sent out to deliver harsh criticism instead of driving change management?

___

___

___

___

No. 38

Acceptance

Team buy-in is the language that defines project success.

Personal Reactions

Agree? Disagree? Seen examples? How would you use this? Date entries, revisit from time to time—sketch if useful!

DOI: 10.4324/9781003507383-47

Guided Inquiry

1. Explore a time when a team believed in change overall but not the project.

____

____

2. How do you check the pulse of your team and coworkers during a project?

____

____

3. With the strain of multiple priorities, how do you keep buy-in alive?

____

____

Exploration

Explore a time when you lost the team. They stopped supporting the project and the need for change. Did it turn around? Could you have done anything differently? Were there warning signs?

____

____

____

____

____

____

No. 39

Elevation

Adding levels below not only distances one from any team, its challenges, and its successes, but also sets you on an ever-teetering perch that can collapse without warning.

After all, the higher something goes, the thinner it becomes.

Build a solid base. And expend every effort to maintain it and never be far from it.

Personal Reactions

Agree? Disagree? Seen examples? How would you use this? Date entries, revisit from time to time—sketch if useful!

DOI: 10.4324/9781003507383-48

Guided Inquiry

1. Have you seen an entity add levels of management? Was it effective?

   ____

   ____

2. How does an executive leader stay close to the bedrock of the company?

   ____

   ____

3. How might adding intermediaries or others negatively impact a leader?

   ____

   ____

Exploration

Have you been in a situation to reduce levels of management? Increase them? What were the driving forces? What about other positions like special advisors, etc.?

____

____

____

____

____

____

No. 40

Impact

A problematic team has a problematic leader.

Personal Reactions

Agree? Disagree? Seen examples? How would you use this? Date entries, revisit from time to time—sketch if useful!

DOI: 10.4324/9781003507383-49

Guided Inquiry

1. Is a leader ever not responsible for their team?

____

____

2. How have you handled issues within a team or a problematic team member?

____

____

3. Have you ever been in a position wherein you replaced a team leader? Why?

____

____

Exploration

What are your top 3–5 strategies for addressing tension in a team? How do you address behavior issues? How do you source the causes of discord? Once addressed, how do you manage backsliding to old behaviors? Have you ever found yourself to be the problem?

____

____

____

____

____

____

No. 41

Role

The practitioner has no place in the team's success, only in its failure.

Personal Reactions

Agree? Disagree? Seen examples? How would you use this? Date entries, revisit from time to time—sketch if useful!

DOI: 10.4324/9781003507383-50

Guided Inquiry

1. Why might a practitioner taking credit for project success be an issue?

____

____

2. Does this idea differ if the team is one of change experts versus laypeople?

____

____

3. How can a practitioner be responsible for a team's failure?

____

____

Exploration

In establishing a change management and operational excellence program, what steps could be taken in program design to make sure teams are celebrated for their success, while outside of the project the practitioner/change agent also experiences the impact of a success engagement? Develop a few program attributes to achieve this.

____

____

____

____

____

Tool: Visualize Everything

Many methodologies in process improvement involve some aspect of visual management regarding operational results and related metrics. Consider also project and operations management and its use of kanban and other charts. How many scrum groups have you seen without a swimlane? I advocate for visualizing EVERYTHING!

Of Kanbans and Swimlanes

I most often use a simple, physical kanban board with the categories of To Do, On Hold, In Progress, and Done. While you could use a digital version, this is only recommended if you have the discipline to view it every day. If it is always visible on a wall-mounted monitor, problem solved! My board is usually on a portion of a whiteboard or even a corkboard. Projects are on cards and move along as progress is made. This approach is geared to my work style: (1) I need forced visual reminder of the projects I am working on, and (2) I need only to know generally where it is in the process as more details can be found elsewhere quickly.

Clearly, more elaborate boards can be made to mirror project milestones such as developing specifications, user testing, and deployment. Don't limit yourself to standard board constructs, but make it work for you and

DOI: 10.4324/9781003507383-51

how you and your team works. Also, always consider such boards to be iterative and allow them to evolve as projects and tasks change and work processes mature.

Using Objects to Ideate and Visualize

There are other methods to track your progress in order to manage tasks, subtasks, and other items, especially while in the moment or even when brainstorming. One method I have used before is to have a set of objects that represent certain tasks. I use a small set of plastic toy soldiers: the radio operator works great for communications issues; the minesweeper for finding hidden issues; the officer ready to recon the area with his binoculars; and the team leader moving the troops forward. There is nothing magic about using plastic soldiers. You could use chess pieces or other items as long as the objects quickly and clearly make sense to you. You can even use stickie notes if you have several steps to organize, similar to a process map.

I often use this visualization technique when I am ideating or developing a plan. I can quickly place these soldiers in order to record how I need to proceed before the idea gets lost in the myriad of details and thoughts I am working through. If the information flow is less hectic and you have more time, this method can be useful in thinking options through and testing iterations before reducing the process to paper.

No. 42

Enmity

Seeing a world of adversaries means you have seen no farther than yourself.

Personal Reactions

Agree? Disagree? Seen examples? How would you use this? Date entries, revisit from time to time—sketch if useful!

DOI: 10.4324/9781003507383-52

Guided Inquiry

1. Why would a leader believe they are surrounded by enemies?

2. The same question, but they are surrounded by people they hold as incompetent.

3. Have you ever worked with someone who had a 'hero complex'? Explain.

Exploration

You're assigned a change management project. A leader is toxic and believes no one, even his own team, is as good or capable as he is. Further, he believes various people are 'out to get him' or make him look bad. He dismisses projects because he feels he has all the answers. You need to meet him, assess the situation, and report back to the board. What do you do? What do you ask? What course of action do you suggest?

No. 43

Control

Anger is the badge of the fool, not the banner of a leader.

Personal Reactions

Agree? Disagree? Seen examples? How would you use this? Date entries, revisit from time to time—sketch if useful!

DOI: 10.4324/9781003507383-53

Guided Inquiry

1. What do staff experience when they see a leader lose their temper?

 ____

 ____

2. Have you ever worked with someone who felt outbursts were 'executive'?

 ____

 ____

3. How do you handle a leader who is constantly angry and subject to outbursts?

 ____

 ____

Exploration

Explore a time when you lost your temper or cool at work. What happened? What were the ramifications? Did you try to address the outcomes? What could you have done differently? Did you learn the behavior from a previous leader? How do you handle employees in the same circumstance?

____

____

____

____

____

____

No. 44

Fault

On the journey of finding fault, the first stop should be you.

Blame is not a method or tool, but the path of the weak and self-possessed.

Acceptance of personal fault is the aegis of a practitioner and the journey taken with the same is the doorstep to a successful career.

Personal Reactions

Agree? Disagree? Seen examples? How would you use this? Date entries, revisit from time to time—sketch if useful!

DOI: 10.4324/9781003507383-54

Guided Inquiry

1. How has your career developed because of mistakes you've made?

____

____

2. Give examples of when you've seen people use blame as a tool.

____

____

3. How do you distinguish between finding a root cause and finding fault?

____

____

Exploration

Let's explore that last question more. How do you define a 'root cause'? How do you define 'fault'? What does finding fault look like? How is this different than finding a root cause of an issue? How do you address the problem and not be negative?

____

____

____

____

____

____

____

No. 45

Manipulation

Traps of intellect or judgment advance no cause for they are the tools with which the over-confident build a bridge to nowhere.

Personal Reactions

Agree? Disagree? Seen examples? How would you use this? Date entries, revisit from time to time—sketch if useful!

DOI: 10.4324/9781003507383-55

Guided Inquiry

1. Have you ever been in a 'gotcha' moment? Explain.

___

___

2. How would you define a trap of intellect? Does this involve hypotheticals?

___

___

3. Explore examples of someone pursuing shortcomings and not results.

___

___

Exploration

What other forms does manipulation take in the world of change management and operational excellence? List 3–5 examples and how they might be mitigated.

___

___

___

___

___

___

___

No. 46

Conceit

Flaunting the nuanced is the path of the arrogant and a failed chance to teach.

Personal Reactions

Agree? Disagree? Seen examples? How would you use this? Date entries, revisit from time to time—sketch if useful!

DOI: 10.4324/9781003507383-56

Guided Inquiry

1. Gives examples of someone making learning more difficult than necessary.

 ____

 ____

2. Some say there is power in 'secret' knowledge. What does this mean to you?

 ____

 ____

3. Have you seen someone use a technicality to attack another's confidence?

 ____

 ____

Exploration

Have you ever critiqued someone's lack of understanding based solely on a nuanced technicality? Did they really understand the issue at a high level, but you took objection and wanted to knock them down a few steps? Why? What happened? Did you fix it?

____

____

____

____

____

No. 47

Substance

You may shout much and shout loudly, but then fear nothing more than when your voice goes hoarse.

Personal Reactions

Agree? Disagree? Seen examples? How would you use this? Date entries, revisit from time to time—sketch if useful!

DOI: 10.4324/9781003507383-57

Guided Inquiry

1. What does bullying look like in the workplace?

___

___

2. Have you experienced an episode of bullying? Explain.

___

___

3. Do you think some people consciously use anger as a tool of leadership?

___

___

Exploration

Have you seen a bully fall from their position? How did it happen? What were the ramifications? Was it part of a change management engagement?

___

___

___

___

___

___

___

___

No. 48

Gossip

The criticism delivered to third parties in secret will make public your shortcomings as a leader.

Personal Reactions

Agree? Disagree? Seen examples? How would you use this? Date entries, revisit from time to time—sketch if useful!

DOI: 10.4324/9781003507383-58

Guided Inquiry

1. How have you handled a covertly critical team member in your career?

2. Ever seen a leader caught off-guard by gossip they spread?

3. When does gossip become dangerous in the workplace? To the change team?

Exploration

Have you seen gossip impact a decision? Did it have a positive or negative impact? If positive, how could it have been handled differently? What are the alternatives to gossip? When is it acceptable to use gossip?

No. 49

Arrogance

In demanding that others look inward while you look only outward is to fail—as a person, as a teacher, and as a leader. Do not hide from yourself.

Personal Reactions

Agree? Disagree? Seen examples? How would you use this? Date entries, revisit from time to time—sketch if useful!

DOI: 10.4324/9781003507383-59

Guided Inquiry

1. What is the difference between arrogance and confidence?

____

____

2. Do you require others to develop themselves but exclude yourself?

____

____

3. Have you used your own mistakes as examples while coaching someone?

____

____

Exploration

How do you set an example for your team, mentees, and others to follow in regard to personal reflection and professional development? Do you have a professional development plan? Do you make time for learning? Do you help others make time? What are your goals? Just remember, what you require of others you should illustrate with yourself.

____

____

____

____

____

____

Tool: Perception Is Your Reality

'There is no truth. There is only perception'.

Gustave Flaubert

'I know that the object I'm looking at is an Egg—but I also know that if it talks to me like a person, it is not an Egg'.

Dr. Hunter S. Thompson

As a change practitioner, you will encounter a variety of forces that seem intent on limiting your success. Issues may be taken with your approach, methods, demeanor, or results, to name a few. These issues may be earned criticisms or simply chaff geared to deflect attention and focus from the mission at hand. Regardless of the source, they are now your reality.

Let's face it—it stinks when someone has a perception of you that isn't true, especially if they are having this perception either because of a misinterpretation or, worse, on purpose and not because of something you actually did.

So, what do you do?

If the perception is based, at least in part, on reality, then you have some work to do. Seek out a mentor, coach, or other trusted feedback partner, and discuss the issue with them. It is fair to do some averaging here

DOI: 10.4324/9781003507383-60

between the perception you were presented with and what your feedback partners see. Then determine what you are going to do both to resolve the present issue and engage in some personal development. If one person has a negative perception of you, it might be worth an apology or at the very least a discussion in a safe space to explore the issue. It might be as simple as explaining your motives behind an action or an event. Conversely, it might be something you are fine with leaving unresolved. Perhaps the perception serves your purposes or there is no resolution possible.

What do you do if the perception is not based on fact? Well, sadly, facts are usually irrelevant in these cases, and there is no court before which to argue them. You may have to do some soul searching as to whether you apologize for something you didn't do or take some other action that to some may appear to validate that the perception was legitimate. Above all, you must make sure that you function as an effective change agent and sometimes allowing the other party to momentarily have power may address the issue. Or perhaps there is a process they want looked at after this project? Or they just need to be reassured they have a role in the entity in the future? Or maybe you just didn't give them the attention they felt they deserved. Be open to possibilities, and explore your options. Remember that efforts to resolve the perception will take up time and resources, which might be the intent of the other party—be mindful and strategic.

No. 50

Waves

The stray comment made whether of fact or bravado can be as uncontrollable as a match to a dry forest.

Take care in what you try to ignite.

Personal Reactions

Agree? Disagree? Seen examples? How would you use this? Date entries, revisit from time to time—sketch if useful!

DOI: 10.4324/9781003507383-61

Guided Inquiry

1. Ever had a comment make it further than you intended?

2. What does a change agent accomplish in bragging on success?

3. What happens when a brag is discovered to be a lie or a factual stretch?

Exploration

What are 3–5 strategies you could use to address a comment or comments that have gotten out of control? How would you provide coaching to address the issue with those responsible?

No. 51

Braggadocio

How impactful can one be when they spend their time shouting about how great they are?

Personal Reactions

Agree? Disagree? Seen examples? How would you use this? Date entries, revisit from time to time—sketch if useful!

DOI: 10.4324/9781003507383-62

Guided Inquiry

1. What is the most impactful measure of change agent success?

____

____

2. Is there a time or venue for the change agent to tout past successes?

____

____

3. What achievement matters most to you as someone involved in change?

____

____

Exploration

Explore a time when you worked with someone whose reputation was based on past stories and not recent results. Did someone intervene? If so, how?

____

____

____

____

____

____

____

No. 52

Ramifications

The-ies one tells form a tornado of sorts, with each falsehood adding strength.

Soon one finds the control they had in designing the lies has created a force that will humble them with terrifying success as it tosses them about.

Personal Reactions

Agree? Disagree? Seen examples? How would you use this? Date entries, revisit from time to time—sketch if useful!

DOI: 10.4324/9781003507383-63

Guided Inquiry

1. Have you worked for or with someone who had 'career fables' or total lies?

___

___

2. What do you do when you catch someone in a lie? Is action even needed?

___

___

3. Have you seen an applicant or coworker bend the truth about successes?

___

___

Exploration

Going deeper on the last question, explore what they were exaggerating and how you knew. Also examine when you realized it and what actions were taken. Were you right? Could you have done something differently?

___

___

___

___

___

___

No. 53

Experience

Practitioners are not made, they develop.

Personal Reactions

Agree? Disagree? Seen examples? How would you use this? Date entries, revisit from time to time—sketch if useful!

DOI: 10.4324/9781003507383-64

Guided Inquiry

1. What value do you place on experience in your training program?

___

___

2. How many completed projects does a practitioner need before leading?

___

___

3. How do you manage professional development in change management?

___

___

Exploration

Was your professional development in change management guided by another? If so, whom? How? Explore the relationship and how you learned the field.

___

___

___

___

___

___

___

No. 54

Learning

To want knowledge is to know thirst.

Understand that water bottles are everywhere.

Personal Reactions

Agree? Disagree? Seen examples? How would you use this? Date entries, revisit from time to time—sketch if useful!

DOI: 10.4324/9781003507383-65

Guided Inquiry

1. Are you a continuous learner? Explain.

2. What fields should the change agent learn about? Why?

3. How do you support team member learning?

Exploration

What was the most unlikely place or source you ended up learning the most from? What did you learn? How? How was it helpful?

No. 55

Coaching

If a plant grows counter to my desired direction, I do not slap or strike it.

I apply gentle pressure and nurture it until it finds its way.

Personal Reactions

Agree? Disagree? Seen examples? How would you use this? Date entries, revisit from time to time—sketch if useful!

DOI: 10.4324/9781003507383-66

Guided Inquiry

1. With a performance issue, do you coach first or punish first? Why?

____

____

2. Have you worked for someone who was quick to punish? Explain.

____

____

3. When is coaching and support not enough?

____

____

Exploration

Have you ever punished someone too much? Why? Did you take steps to resolve the mistake or move on? How did the team member react?

____

____

____

____

____

____

____

____

____

Tool: PIN Feedback

Finding a system to deliver feedback can help you make sure your words land with the proper intent. Some propose a system called PIN, which stands for Positive, Interesting, and Negative. I don't care for the 'N', especially since negativity is what we are trying to avoid. I prefer a different last element. Here is the PIN I use:

Positive—What they did that was great. Give 2–3 examples.
Interesting—This can be either something they did or information they presented.
Notes for Next Time—These is where you make critiques with solid example.

Example scenario: A team member just delivered a briefing to get senior management up to speed on the issues the company had been experiencing in loading trucks during the afternoon shift. The presentation was informative, made a mountain of data relatable by using visuals, but went over time and had a many, many slides. Here is your feedback:

Positive: 'Great job! You got the issues across and how you validated them. Further, your solutions are well within budget and show empathy to the warehouse team'.

DOI: 10.4324/9781003507383-67

Interesting: 'I have never seen a spaghetti diagram be animated and include time data. That was impactful and brought the issue to life'.
Notes for Next Time: 'The presentation went over schedule by like 15 minutes. It is not a big issue, but we need to make sure we respect the leadership team's time. Next time, let's try fewer slides and see where that gets us'.

No. 56

Introspection

Suggesting feedback must be like a shared road, accept the flow or else the way becomes useless or dangerous to all.

Personal Reactions

Agree? Disagree? Seen examples? How would you use this? Date entries, revisit from time to time—sketch if useful!

DOI: 10.4324/9781003507383-68

Guided Inquiry

1. Explain a time you received feedback you didn't want.

2. Have you worked with someone who liked to give but not receive feedback?

3. When does feedback cause negativity?

Exploration

What are your best practices for delivering feedback? Are they effective? Do you use different approaches for different situations or people?

No. 57

Growth

If you dodge critique and coaching as deftly as a punch or kick, you simply magnify the pain of a future impact.

Personal Reactions

Agree? Disagree? Seen examples? How would you use this? Date entries, revisit from time to time—sketch if useful!

DOI: 10.4324/9781003507383-69

Guided Inquiry

1. Why would someone dodge attempts by others to help them?

____

____

2. What happens in your career when you avoid any assessment or feedback?

____

____

3. How do you deliver critique in a project team and maintain buy-in/positivity?

____

____

Exploration

How have you seen people avoid critique, feedback, or coaching? Any ideas as to their motives in dodging? How did it work out for them?

____

____

____

____

____

____

____

No. 58

Power

Understand the power of 'we' over the weakness of 'I'.

Personal Reactions

Agree? Disagree? Seen examples? How would you use this? Date entries, revisit from time to time—sketch if useful!

DOI: 10.4324/9781003507383-70

Guided Inquiry

1. How have you dealt with a team member trying to control the team?

2. How do you support diversity of thought and efforts in managing change?

3. Can a team really produce a higher quality product than an individual?

Exploration

Re-read 'Know Your Path'. How, if at all, do elements of that message relate to building and working with a team? Can teamwork be seen as a path itself?

No. 59

Ownership

The most powerful force and the most humbling force are the same—responsibility.

Personal Reactions

Agree? Disagree? Seen examples? How would you use this? Date entries, revisit from time to time—sketch if useful!

DOI: 10.4324/9781003507383-71

Guided Inquiry

1. What does 'responsibility' mean to you?

____

____

2. Do you see it as a benefit or a burden?

____

____

3. Can you drive lasting change without responsibility?

____

____

Exploration

Dive deeper in Question 3. If you need responsibility, how much? If leading a team, do you shelter them from the negative consequences and let them have the rewards?

____

____

____

____

____

____

____

____

No. 60

Stewardship

Stewardship is the pinnacle of leadership.

It is judgment free.

It makes us selfless.

It gives us a sense of purpose.

It assigns us a duty.

Personal Reactions

Agree? Disagree? Seen examples? How would you use this? Date entries, revisit from time to time—sketch if useful!

DOI: 10.4324/9781003507383-72

Guided Inquiry

1. Have you heard of the concept of stewardship before in leadership? Where?

2. How can putting the organization first focus a team?

3. As a change agent, have you left places better than you found them?

Exploration

Explore the concept of stewardship as a way to build a team. How does stewardship support cohesion and sense of purpose? Does it make results more meaningful and understandable?

Tool: The Right Fit

Sometimes, for whatever reason, we find ourselves in the wrong place. The wrong job, wrong team, wrong project, wrong title, wrong whatever. This can cause stress, which in turn causes performance and mood issues. An employee or team may act out because they feel trapped and are at their emotional limit. When I come across folks experiencing a previously uncustomary performance slump, I look for causes, which usually entails a chat. I say I've noticed some issues and want to talk over the situation and not the issues. I tell them I've been in stressful situations that impacted my performance and it is ok to admit when you're there. I ask if they are happy with their duties or are interested in something else. I also ask if they happy with the team or entity and see if they want a career change. These conversations have resolved so many issues and helped folks find peace.

So, what do you do about yourself? Does an offered promotion fit with how you see your career? Does the offer allow you to move down your path or see a new future to which you begin to craft a new path? Newness is always attractive at first. However, when the shine wears off, is the opportunity still a gift or has it become a howling banshee calling for your soul? A useful test is the following:

1. Even on its worst day, when your boss, partners, employees, and even the public are mad at your endeavor, would you still want to be in the offered position?

DOI: 10.4324/9781003507383-73

2. More still, do you believe that not only should you be in the position under such an eventuality, there is no one else who should be there BUT you?

These questions are a test of fortitude, humility, and courage. Sometimes the best answer to both is a frank and clear, 'No'. Being honest with yourself is a tremendous gift. Even if you answer 'Yes' to both, you can still be scared. That just shows you gave the right answers. I fear someone who answers in the affirmative to both and has no anxiety or inner doubt. That person will crash and crash hard. These crashes can endanger employees and the organization. By embracing your self-doubt and fear of failure, you will push beyond your comfort zone. Working at the edge of your comfort zone is the only way to develop and improve yourself. Without pushing, there is no progress. Keep these concepts in mind when dealing with that problematic employee, team member, or even leader. Empathy is a solid place to start with many situations.

No. 61

Journey

The goal of change is improvement. Or put another way, simple betterment.

Make sure you have left the entity improved, then celebrate the distance traveled.

Personal Reactions

Agree? Disagree? Seen examples? How would you use this? Date entries, revisit from time to time—sketch if useful!

DOI: 10.4324/9781003507383-74

Guided Inquiry

1. Have you seen results celebrated before they were earned or realized?

2. What do you do when leadership wants you to push further than the solution?

3. How do you measure improvement?

Exploration

Is there a direct correlation between project efforts and outcomes? Can a simple decision have an epic impact? Can a months-long project make only small changes? Is one necessarily better than the other? How do you assess this?

No. 62

Readiness

It will never be the perfect situation. You will never have all the support, authority, or resources you need.

But know this, no one has ever had these and yet lasting, meaningful change has happened.

In fact, such deficiencies are the truest drivers of change.

Personal Reactions

Agree? Disagree? Seen examples? How would you use this? Date entries, revisit from time to time—sketch if useful!

DOI: 10.4324/9781003507383-75

Guided Inquiry

1. When were you asked to achieve a lot but were given little to get it done?

   ____

   ____

2. As a change agent, what are the top 3–5 drivers of change you see regularly?

   ____

   ____

3. How does seeing what's missing clue you in on the changes needed?

   ____

   ____

Exploration

Time for another old, yet versatile tool: Force Field Analysis. Explore how FFA can be used to understand the results expected versus resources available. How much change can you readily achieve? This will take editing the tool a bit, but this book contains a page that helps!

____

____

____

____

____

____

Tool: 'Firefighting'—Rapid Reaction Change

Firefighting

Change management and improvement efforts often result from an operational issue or even a failure/crisis. In responding quickly, the simplest strategy is the best as you may need a team with diverse operational skillsets but who may lack training in process improvement or change management. Often, such efforts are called 'firefighting', which is more appropriate than it may seem. Firefighting offers a simple approach that can be modified to provide an expedient and effective strategy for responding to an improvement situation. In firefighting, this approach has three fronts: Cooling, Removal of Resources, and Smothering. Now, let's modify this to our purposes.

Cooling

In a fire, you have to remove heat. The operational issue is no different. Heat may come in the form of:

DOI: 10.4324/9781003507383-76

- Failure to meet performance expectations
- Stakeholder attitudes (including anger, jealousy, and shame)
- Management attention
- Media attention
- Previously failed improvement efforts
- Stresses such as budget, market pressures, material issues, and difficulty securing a dependable and/or skilled workforce.
- Entity structural or leadership changes.

It is important to note that 'heat' can come from inside and outside the process and from inside and outside the team, department, or company. There is no such thing as a closed system anymore and the integration of operations increases the sources of heat on the operational issue.

As with a fire, total and absolute removal of the heat may not be possible or even needed. What is needed is lowering the level of heat. In a process setting, this removes pressures that may block developing a more successful resolution to the issue. A stressed team under constant pressure will become fuel for the fire, not a tool against it. Treat the sources of heat as constraints and make a list. What pressures are in play? How can these sources be mitigated? Approaches can be simple or complex, depending on what is needed. Possibilities include:

- Access to resources, such as overtime, financial resources, or other items.
- In-person, clearly stated support to the change team from the most senior leader possible.
- Temporary reporting structure to a senior leader capable of removing roadblocks and providing resources.
- Communication with stakeholders, especially crucial conversations.
- Performance management of staff, focused on coaching and development, but perhaps including reassignment or termination.

Perhaps, too, it is time to simply cut a service or product. Something that has outlasted its usefulness can cause a lot of problems and generate a lot of heat.

Removal of Resources

For our purposes, this might best be seen as simply Resources, with removal or addition of such being part of the solution. This is an excellent way to look at process inputs. What input is derailing the endeavor? Once you find it, ask if it is necessary. If not, dump it. It's like limiting the fuel available to a fire. Maybe it is time to change suppliers or vendors. Maybe it is time for a piece of equipment to be replaced.

Smothering

In firefighting, smothering is an effort to reduce oxygen available to a fire. For operational improvement and change management, smothering tackles the single most explosive element in a bad process or damaging behavior—lack consistent, surrounding attention. Encapsulate the issue. Make sure its badness does not bleed over. A bad process, negative team, or other issue can easily bleed over and cause havoc elsewhere. Once something is in the wild, it will change and it could get out of control. So, smother. Lock it down, isolate it, and send in a team empowered with authority and given resources to resolve the issue. And never let up. The push to fix it must be constant. Any signs of weakness will allow a flare up and will scorch the entire effort.

After Action

Once you've gained control and made some improvements, you can always double back and dig in with more complex change methodologies to make sure all issues have been solved in a lasting manner if needed.

Practitioners and management often believe that change management and process improvement are not agile and take a lot of time. This isn't the case. Make sure your approaches are as flexible and nimble as the environments in which they operate.

No. 63

Character

No matter the toll paid or the scars that remain, always be magnanimous in victory.

Personal Reactions

Agree? Disagree? Seen examples? How would you use this? Date entries, revisit from time to time—sketch if useful!

DOI: 10.4324/9781003507383-77

Guided Inquiry

1. Do you handle success honorably?

2. How do you celebrate a change without celebrating someone's failure?

3. How do you handle success when others thought it was unlikely/impossible?

Exploration

When has a project, engagement, or assignment taken a toll on you? What happened? Was it worth it? Did you recover? How? Did the experience give you any lessons learned or new coping strategies?

No. 64

Ripples

Once you do something, it is like tossing a rock in a pond, the ripples travel far beyond your point of action.

Personal Reactions

Agree? Disagree? Seen examples? How would you use this? Date entries, revisit from time to time—sketch if useful!

DOI: 10.4324/9781003507383-78

Guided Inquiry

1. What is the difference between tactical and strategic decision-making?

2. Explore a time when someone failed to consider a 'ripple' of an action taken.

3. In a project, how do you limit the ripples? Can you? Should you?

Exploration

Based on your change role and the entity you work for, develop a tool to predict and mitigate the ripples from a change management decision or project. Once developed, try it out and see if it helps manage intended and unintended outcomes.

No. 65

Questioning

Always question the 'why' of things. What are the reasons and the motives? What happens if we succeed? What happens if we fail?

Personal Reactions

Agree? Disagree? Seen examples? How would you use this? Date entries, revisit from time to time—sketch if useful!

DOI: 10.4324/9781003507383-79

Guided Inquiry

1. How do you assess the motives/reasons of leadership suggesting a project?

   ____

   ____

2. Do you consider possible failure in planning a project? How?

   ____

   ____

3. Can a successful project actually have a negative impact? How?

   ____

   ____

Exploration

Examine a time when you were sent to fix a process, but the issue really addressed was something different. Have you ever taken a project only to find it wasn't a process or practice that needed fixing?

No. 66

Evolution

Once words become action, your ability to influence the outcomes wanes exponentially. Exercise caution.

Personal Reactions

Agree? Disagree? Seen examples? How would you use this? Date entries, revisit from time to time—sketch if useful!

DOI: 10.4324/9781003507383-80

Guided Inquiry

1. Why is it easier to control words versus actions? Or is it?

____

____

2. What happens when a project transitions too quickly from ideation to action?

____

____

3. How do change management decisions evolve in the real world?

____

____

Exploration

Consider applying this concept to team issues. What can happen when words (or perhaps gossip) lead to an action (removal, coaching, etc.)? What if the gossip is just that and you validated it only because you took action?

____

____

____

____

____

____

____

No. 67

People

Always start with giving a damn about your people.

Nothing happens without them.

Personal Reactions

Agree? Disagree? Seen examples? How would you use this? Date entries, revisit from time to time—sketch if useful!

DOI: 10.4324/9781003507383-81

Guided Inquiry

1. How do you show support for your team?

2. Explore a time when a leader alienated their team. What happened?

3. Can a change agent be effective alone, working without a team?

Exploration

If your team picked 3–5 words to describe you, what do you think those words would be? Now, go ask them.

No. 68

Action

Never deal with an opponent on their ground. Make them step first. Make them approach you. Then, take advantage of the momentum.

Personal Reactions

Agree? Disagree? Seen examples? How would you use this? Date entries, revisit from time to time—sketch if useful!

DOI: 10.4324/9781003507383-82

Guided Inquiry

1. How have you dealt with enemies of change?

2. If an opponent makes the first move, why is this valuable?

3. How might an opponent attempt to influence your project?

Exploration

How do you attempt to make an opponent a proponent? Could the same person hold the different roles depending on the project or initiative? Do you believe you have encountered a true adversarial opponent before?

No. 69

Honesty

Regard and respect are expressed through honesty. Whether it is good news or bad, be fair, be clear, be understanding, and be honest.

Personal Reactions

Agree? Disagree? Seen examples? How would you use this? Date entries, revisit from time to time—sketch if useful!

DOI: 10.4324/9781003507383-83

Guided Inquiry

1. How have you been impacted by the dishonesty of someone else?

2. How do you deliver bad news when working on a project?

3. How might someone engage in dishonesty but not be malicious in doing so?

Exploration

Explore a situation in which someone did not come to appreciate your honesty until much later. What happened? How did they come to appreciate it?

No. 70

Protection

Shield your team from attack. While they are making progress, you are deflecting the arrows.

Personal Reactions

Agree? Disagree? Seen examples? How would you use this? Date entries, revisit from time to time—sketch if useful!

DOI: 10.4324/9781003507383-84

Guided Inquiry

1. Why might a project team or a lone change agent need top cover?

2. How do you safeguard the teams you're working with?

3. Who might attack a team or change agent? How?

Exploration

Conflict resolution techniques, especially de-escalation, are pivotal for change agents. Find either in-person, online, or both training sessions. Complete the courses and be prepared for your next conflict!

No. 71

Team

A leader in front of or above their people is alone. A leader standing with their people has a team.

Personal Reactions

Agree? Disagree? Seen examples? How would you use this? Date entries, revisit from time to time—sketch if useful!

DOI: 10.4324/9781003507383-85

Guided Inquiry

1. Are you a working leader (meaning you manage and do project work)?

2. How do you assess leaders who elevate themselves over others?

3. Is rank ever valuable? Explain.

Exploration

How often do you reflect on your leadership style? Do you ever make changes? Explain. Is your style the same for all situations? How do you describe your style of leadership?

No. 72

Practice

Empower all to question everything.

Personal Reactions

Agree? Disagree? Seen examples? How would you use this? Date entries, revisit from time to time—sketch if useful!

DOI: 10.4324/9781003507383-86

Guided Inquiry

1. Can change happen without questioning?

2. Are there problems with leadership being questioned by those they supervise?

3. How do you turn questions into projects and change initiatives?

Exploration

When was the last time you questioned a leader's decision? What was the decision? What did you question? What happened?

Tool: Change Perspective

A process, series of processes, action, or behavior can be seen as a force moving in a direction and sometimes that direction is counter to the desired outcome. Now, tradition would dictate that meeting it head-on and countering the force would mitigate the undesirable and drive change. This can have its place, but know that there is an inherently valuable tool in your arsenal for such situations: perspective. A master knife instructor once taught me that the critical moves in surviving a knife attack were a blocking motion to protect your vital areas and a shove and lateral movement to disengage. Linear movement is in the favor of the attacker. Lateral movement gets you clear of immediate harm, makes your attacker turn, and gives you time to escape or counterattack. Let's look at a different example that illustrates the point.

Let's say our 26th president, Theodore Roosevelt, has just donned his pith helmet for an evening stroll and comes across some primeval beast in the woods of the Amazon. Searching his pockets, he finds his notebook and a pencil. Clearly, there are only three options (if you see a fourth, namely running away, shame on you!). Option 1 is to sketch the head-on view he has of the beast. Option 2 involves him making a lateral move left, where he can see the rest of the animal and sketch away. Or Option 3, he makes a lateral move right and sketches all the same. But without moving laterally, the only perspective is limited in accuracy and options. While his head-on drawing would be accurate, it is only so from that perspective

DOI: 10.4324/9781003507383-87

and misses the rest of the issue, which could hide a bigger problem! This works for solutions as well. What if this beast was less than friendly and Theodore Roosevelt found himself unarmed. Sure, he could go hands on, but what if by going left he found a rock or by going right he found a sturdy stick. Perspective informs every move of improvement.

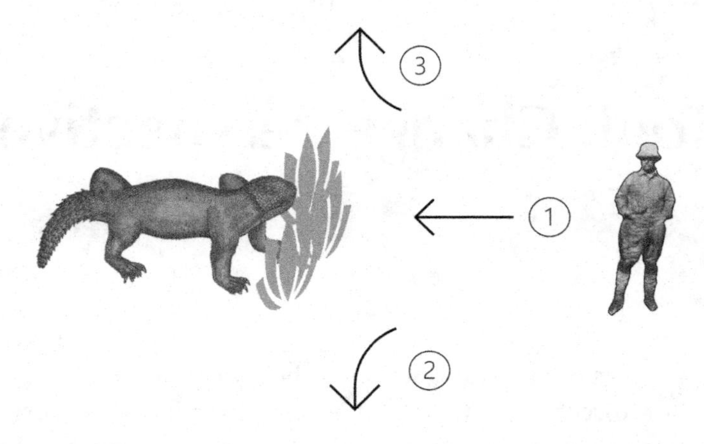

During a process improvement project or similar engagement, you can get a better angle on the issue by including staff from other divisions who have no experience with the process—it's likely they will see things those more familiar might miss. Also include those upstream and downstream from the focus of the process team. Using the previously mentioned empathy map can also help provide different vantage points on the problem at hand. And when it comes to testing solutions, an outside perspective can be the key to a solid poke yoke of the new process.

No. 73

Accessibility

Accessibility is the super power of a successful leader.

Personal Reactions

Agree? Disagree? Seen examples? How would you use this? Date entries, revisit from time to time—sketch if useful!

DOI: 10.4324/9781003507383-88

Guided Inquiry

1. What does 'accessible' mean to you?

2. Is a relatable leader more effective than a one perceived as being distant?

3. Does accessibility get leaders closer to the root causes of problems?

Exploration

What must a leader do to be accessible? What level is too much? How do you manage it?

No. 74

Commands

Issuing commands only burdens you with endless decisions.

Personal Reactions

Agree? Disagree? Seen examples? How would you use this? Date entries, revisit from time to time—sketch if useful!

DOI: 10.4324/9781003507383-89

Guided Inquiry

1. Are you good at delegating work? Explain.

___

___

2. Have you worked with someone who felt they had the only right answer?

___

___

3. How do you decide it's your decision versus belonging to a direct report?

___

___

Exploration

How do you coach and mentor a direct report, especially a manager or supervisor who tries to get you or others to make decisions for them? Have you seen someone make bad decisions so that they were absolved of that responsibility?

___

___

___

___

___

___

No. 75

Effort

Knowledge is sometimes shared to brag. Effort is always shared to support and achieve.

Personal Reactions

Agree? Disagree? Seen examples? How would you use this? Date entries, revisit from time to time—sketch if useful!

DOI: 10.4324/9781003507383-90

Guided Inquiry

1. How do you handle the team member who talks a lot but does nothing?

2. Why is effort a valuable contribution?

3. When is knowledge sharing a valuable effort?

Exploration

How do you assess and manage the contribution level of team members? Of project sponsors? Of yourself?

No. 76

Advancement

While losing a practitioner provides short-term sorrow, an expanded arena for their skills builds a new world.

Personal Reactions

Agree? Disagree? Seen examples? How would you use this? Date entries, revisit from time to time—sketch if useful!

DOI: 10.4324/9781003507383-91

Guided Inquiry

1. What do you do when a valued team member or leader moves on?

2. Looking back at the last 2–3 years, where have your trainees gone if they left?

3. How do you recruit for change agents and practitioners?

Exploration

This is reflection #76. Now, go write #77.

Index

Printed in the United States
by Baker & Taylor Publisher Services